Goodnight AGGIELAND®

Written by Mark and Cimbrey Brannan
Illustrated by Matt Gardner

AMP&RSAND, INC.

Chicago • New Orleans

ISBN 978-145070625-4

Design: David Robson, Robson Design

Published by
AMPERSAND, INC.
1050 North State Street
Chicago, Illinois 60610

———

203 Finland Place
New Orleans, Louisiana 70131

———

www.ampersandworks.com

———

Printed in U.S.A.

2nd Edition
2 4 6 8 10 9 7 5 3

**To request a personalized copy
or to schedule a book signing/school reading, email
goodnightaggieland@gmail.com**

Dedicated to our son, Zane Addisu—

Ethiopian by birth, Texas Aggie by the grace of God.

There is a place called Aggieland

HOME OF THE 12TH MAN

Where the 12th Man at attention stands

The Wrecking Crew wears Maroon and White

And Yell Leaders holler FIGHT, FIGHT, FIGHT!!!

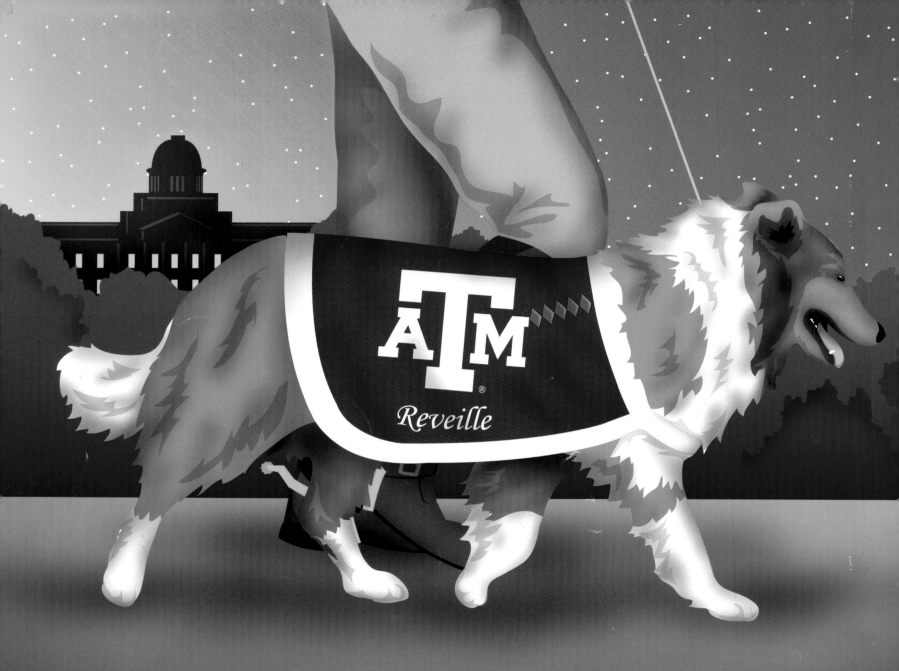

When Reveille barks students get out of class

And folks say "Gig 'Em" and "Howdy" as they pass

As all head to bed after saying goodnight

Let dreams of becoming an Aggie take flight

Goodnight Maroon, Goodnight White

Goodnight Fish Camp and traditions learned right

Goodnight Yell Leaders and Ross Volunteers

Goodnight Cavalry as we cover our ears

Goodnight fighter jets flying over the fans

Goodnight Fightin' Texas Aggie Band

Goodnight Kyle Field and a touchdown pass

Goodnight Fish Pond and a game winning splash

Goodnight Quad and the Corps of Cadets

Goodnight Reed Rowdies and the swish of the nets

Goodnight Olsen Field and the loud student section

Goodnight 41 and your Presidential collection

Goodnight Century Tree with branches so low

Goodnight Sul Ross and pennies stacked in a row

Goodnight Freshmen Spurs, goodnight Senior Boots

Goodnight pass backs and spirited whooooops!

Goodnight Aggie ring and Ring Dance fun

Goodnight Elephant Walk – senior year is half done

Goodnight Silver Taps played low, long and clear

Goodnight Aggie Muster where loved ones call, "Here"

Goodnight Midnight Yell as they turn out the lights

And pull someone close for a sweet kiss goodnight

AGGIE ARCHIVE

Texas A&M University Founded in 1876, the first public university in Texas and one of the nation's largest, committed to "developing leaders of character dedicated to serving the greater good."

Aggie Ring The distinctive symbolic link to the Aggie Network of former students that all Aggies receive upon graduation. The first ring was designed in 1889, revised in 1894, and has been unchanged since then.

Century Tree If a couple walks under this oldest tree on campus, it is certain they will marry. If a proposal takes place here, the marriage is sure to last forever.

Corps of Cadets Comprised of more than 2000, the largest uniformed body in the U.S. outside of the military academies. Called "The Keepers of the Spirit" as many cherished A&M traditions grew out of the Corps.

Elephant Walk Held the week of the football game against the University of Texas, seniors link arms and "wander aimlessly" on campus to remember their time at school. The term originated when one observer noted that they "Looked like elephants, about to die."

Fightin' Texas Aggie Band Comprised of Corps of Cadets members, it is the largest military marching band in the U.S., nationally acclaimed for its precision and style.

Fish Camp Each year 900 counselors welcome Freshmen to a four-day orientation program in East Texas to teach Aggie Traditions and leadership skills and to forge lasting friendships.

Fish Pond After a win at Kyle Field, freshmen Corps members capture the Yell Leaders and carry them to the Fish Pond where they are dunked and lead yell practice for the next week's opponent.

Freshman Spurs Originally, the week of the SMU football game, and later the Texas Tech game, freshmen in the Corps are seen around campus with home-made bottle cap spurs on their shoes symbolizing their desire to "spur" the Mustangs or Red Raiders.

George H. W. Bush Library The presidential library of the 41st U.S. President. Located on 90 acres on the west campus of Texas A&M University.

Gig 'Em At a 1930 game vs. TCU, a dedicated fan and member of the Board of Regents, Pinky Downs '06, yelled "What are we going to do to those Horned Frogs?" Referring to a sharp frog hunting tool, he yelled, "Gig 'Em!" while giving a "thumbs-up." All Aggies continue to use the phrase and sign today as their rally cry.

Howdy Official greeting of all Aggies and a reflection of the welcoming spirit of Aggieland.

Kyle Field Home to the Texas Aggie football team since 1904 and now one of the nation's largest stadiums with a capacity of over 90,000. In 1899 horticulture professor Edwin Jackson Kyle donated land designated for his department and spent $650 out of his own pocket to buy the first 500-seat grandstand.

Midnight Yell Held the night before every home game, over 25,000 current and former students (The 12th Man) join Yell Leaders and the Fightin' Texas Aggie Band to sing the War Hymn, practice their "old army yells" and hear how the Aggies are going to beat the opponent the next day.

Muster A tradition that joins past and present Aggies by recognizing those who have died in the past year. Held every April 21st since 1883, former students gather for the "Roll Call for the Absent" and answer "Here" as names are called to show that each Aggie is present in spirit.

Olsen Field Home to Aggie baseball, the stadium was built in 1978 and named after 1923 graduate, Pat Olsen, a member of the New York Yankees farm system.

Parson's Mounted Cavalry The only mounted cavalry in the United States.

Reed Rowdies The official name of the raucous student section supporting Aggie basketball at Reed arena.

Reveille The First Lady of Aggieland and official mascot of Texas A&M. She is the highest ranking member of the Corps of Cadets and attends class and other campus events with the cadet who cares for her. If Reveille barks while attending class, it is dismissed immediately.

Ring Dance An event held for the Senior Class representing the milestone where they are able to turn their class ring from facing themselves to facing the world.

Ross Volunteers An elite Corps unit that serves as the official honor guard for the Governor of Texas. The RVs also fire a three volley salute during Silver Taps to honor currently enrolled students who have died.

Senior Boots As a member of the Corps of Cadets climbs the ranks, certain privileges are granted, the greatest being presentation of the prized Senior Boots.

Silver Taps The final tribute for any current student that has passed away during the previous month. The ceremony is held at 10:30 pm in front of Sul Ross in the Academic Plaza the first Tuesday of the month. All lights on campus are extinguished, the bells from Albritton tower ring, students gather silently, and buglers play a special rendition of Silver taps three times: once to the north, south, and west. Taps is not played to the east as the sun will never rise on that Aggie again.

Sul Ross Lawrence "Sul" Ross saved the school from closure in the 1890s. Legend is that "Sully" tutored students but would only accept a penny for his thoughts. Today pennies are stacked at the feet of his statue by students wishing for good luck during exams.

The 12th Man While playing Centre College in 1922, the Aggies suffered many injuries. With only 11 players remaining, Coach Dana X. Bible asked E. King Gill to come down from the stands and get ready to play. Gill didn't play, but was the last man on the sideline— the 12th Man. The Aggies won, and since that day, Aggies stand at games, ready and willing to support their team.

Wrecking Crew Name for the Aggie football team's defense coined by defensive back, Chet Brooks, during Coach R.C. Slocum's tenure. It is still chanted today following outstanding defensive performances.

Yell Leaders Aggies have yells, not cheers. Yell Leaders use "Pass Backs" to communicate "old army yells" all the way to the back of the stadium.

THE SPIRIT OF AGGIELAND

Some may boast of prowess bold
Of the school they think so grand
But there's a spirit can ne'er be told
It's the Spirit of Aggieland

Chorus
We are the Aggies, the Aggies are we
True to each other as Aggies can be
We've got to fight, boys
We've got to fight!
We've got to fight for Maroon and White

After they've boosted all the rest
Then they will come and join the best
For we are the Aggies, the Aggies are we
We're from Texas AMC

Second Chorus
T-E-X-A-S-A-G-G-I-E
Fight! Fight! Fight-fight-fight!
Fight, Maroon! And White-white-white!
A-G-G-I-E
Texas! Texas! A-M-C
Gig 'em! Aggies! 1-2-3!
Farmers fight! Farmers fight!
Fight! Fight!
Farmers, farmers, fight!

THE AGGIE WAR HYMN

Hullabaloo, Caneck! Caneck!
Hullabaloo, Caneck! Caneck!

First Verse
All hail to dear old Texas A&M
Rally around Maroon and White
Good luck to dear old Texas Aggies
They are the boys who show the real old fight
That good old Aggie spirit thrills us
And makes us yell and yell and yell
So let's fight for dear old Texas A&M
We're going to beat you all to
Chig-gar-roo-gar-rem
Chig-gar-roo-gar-rem
Rough Tough! Real Stuff! Texas A&M!

Second Verse
Good-bye to texas university
So long to the orange and the white
Good luck to dear old Texas Aggies
They are the boys that show the real old fight
"The eyes of Texas are upon you . . ."
That is the song they sing so well
So good-bye to texas university
We're going to beat you all to
Chig-gar-roo-gar-rem
Chig-gar-roo-gar-rem
Rough Tough! Real Stuff! Texas A&M!